These poems were written while I was going
through cancer treatments 2004–2008.

Many thanks to my family –
my husband Richard
and my daughters Kimberlee and Melissa –
and to my friends and caregivers.
I hope you know how very special you are.
I love you.

Marsha Gullo Frerichs

POWER OF HOPE

ONE WOMAN'S JOURNEY
THROUGH CANCER

By Marsha Gullo Frerichs

Altamesa Press

ACKNOWLEDGEMENT
BY RICHARD FRERICHS, EDITOR

In editing and publishing my wife Marsha's poems, subsequent to her death in 2008, I am deeply grateful to Barbara Buckman Strasko, the first Poet Laureate of Lancaster County, Pennsylvania, for her inspiration to embark on this project. Sincerest thanks also to my publisher and editorial adviser Anthony Bladon of Altamesa Press.

The poems themselves acknowledge many friends, named and unnamed, who provided comfort and support to Marsha through her journey. To Marsha's physicians, Dr. Bruce Brod, Dr. Daleela Dodge and Dr. Joan Kane, I would like to add my own special word of gratitude.

ISBN 1-978-1-300-80690-5

POWER OF HOPE

ONE WOMAN'S JOURNEY
THROUGH CANCER

TABLE OF CONTENTS

THE NEWS

It is not something you read in the headlines of a paper
– The newspaper.
It is not something you see on the six o'clock news
– The news report.
But it is so important to your world,
The phone call from your doctor
– Your news.

You cannot see his face but you hear it in his voice
– The news anchor.
You interrupt before he even speaks,
"Is it good news or bad news?"
One word, three letters.

You take a deep breath, a part of your heart breaks
But you do not let the news shatter your spirit.
You regroup, you shed a tear and you pray
God will be close as you break the news.

The hardest thing in life
Is to tell the ones you love the news report,
When you wish all you had to talk about
Are traveling conditions and the weather.

SHOULD I SHARE?

Should I share my innermost feelings?
Should I write them in poetry and verse?
It is hard to even acknowledge the thoughts,
But God knows them already.

Should I share my fears and doubts and questions?
You are not to worry and then
That nothing turns into something.

I'll fight with all my strength and with prayer
Not to be bald and thin and gray
With lusterless eyes of no hope – the living dead.
Let me embrace life and death with color and laughter,
With open arms holding onto the passion of each day.

Yes, I should share, for in an instant
My gray and beige
Have turned to red and orange and blue and green,
My tears to joyful smiles and my whimpering
To shouts of praise.

Should I share? Yes, this is my purpose.
Yes, I'll share – I'll share my story
With any listening ear.

I'M OK

I smile at people. I walk tall.
I breathe deeply. I laugh a lot.
I appreciate the world around me.
I love life. Yes, I love life.

A few words spoken from my doctor
Will not change me.
I feel the same, I act the same, I still love life.
Only I can change how I feel.

God has given me that control.
No one can take away my passion and my heart.
They are mine forever.
Yes, I love life and I'm OK.

C

What is cancer?
It's the big "C".
It's the one word that is always whispered.
It's life-altering cells.

It's the physical changing of a body.
It's the plague of existence.
It's what scientists are researching,
Trying to find their "C" – the cure.

It touches everyone someday, somehow, someway.
But it is only a word – or is it?

FAITH

Putting your faith in God is like
Releasing the heaviest weight
That has been on your chest.

It is like taking off in a jet,
Soaring into the sky,
But there is no plane.

It is like looking into the night with a billion stars
Only to find you are one of them.

It is like opening your eyes for the first time
And seeing all the colors God created
In a single rainbow.

It is like lying in a field of daisies and
Every flower ends with
"He loves me," yes "He loves me."

9-1-1

Asking Jesus to be your savior
Gives hope to the most hopeless of situations.
He doesn't promise to take away your pain or sorrow;
Both will always exist.
Somehow they are the forces
That turn your face towards heaven.

He hears your cries and your calls for help.
God has your attention.
The dialog is opened.

HOLDING HANDS

Between children,
Holding hands is a sign of friendship.
With a parent and a child,
Holding hands is love, security, and safety.

Between future lovers,
It is a first step showing affection.
Between a husband and a wife,
Holding hands can be a most intimate touch,
Symbolizing the bond of years of love together.

When you are faced with medical problems and testing,
You are very lucky to have someone's hand to hold.
When a spouse or a friend grabs your hand in support,
You know that you are not alone.

The assisting nurse or technician squeezes your hand,
Encouraging you,
Sharing the pain, easing the fears,
Communicating all will be OK.
She is here.

Don't underestimate the gift you give
When you take someone's hand in yours.

MAMMOGRAMS

Mammogram day. My favorite day.

I remember to take two Tylenol
To help alleviate the pain.
Your breast is clamped down,
Smashed, and squeezed just a little more.

Just so it is evened out,
They do the procedure in all directions.
You are asked to hold your breath and stay still.
Who could move?

One down, one to go.
When you are finished you wait, you nervously wait.
If you are lucky you get to go home right away.

TIME

The dermatologist sends you for a simple procedure.
The surgeon reads the pathology report.
The report is faxed to the oncologist.
The oncologist talks to the radiologist.

They are all discussing
How to keep me alive, to give me the most time.

But where is God in this equation?
Has he been sent the fax?
Isn't He the ultimate timekeeper?

So you talk to Him and ask
For His grace and healing and time.

I would like more time.
Time to see graduations and careers,
Time to see weddings and grandchildren,
Time to hold onto my family and friends.
More time to love them and to love life.

God answers me.
"Love is the key. Love is the answer.
Yes, I will give you your time,
Time to fall in love with me."

HAIR TODAY, GONE TOMORROW

What happened to that perfect body of youth?
The bikini has long been packed away.
Sure, there are the extra pounds. They are expected.
Few have the discipline to keep them off.

But what are all these scars and the lopsidedness?
What is this calendar filled with doctor appointments?
What are all these tests and treatments?
Treatments that turn you red.
Chemicals that kill the hair follicles.

Well, you laugh. "Bald is beautiful."
Look at all the shaved heads in this world.
GI Jane was a star.
Here's a joke – it's "hair today and gone tomorrow."
You laugh again, because if you cannot laugh,
The only thing left is to cry.

CANCER WILL NEVER

Cancer might distort the body
But it will never have the ability to...
Ruin my day,
Take away my smile,
Quiet my laughter.

Cancer will never have the power to...
Diminish my love for my family,
Make me question my faith in God
Or end the promise of eternal life.

Cancer will never win the battle because. . .
It cannot, will not and never will have the strength
To beat me emotionally and spiritually.
I am the winner.

TO WAR

There it is in the distance,
A brick wall, a fortress.
War is about to begin.
The enemy is within my body,
An enemy that cannot touch the heart or soul.

HELPERS

Surgeons lend their healing hands.
The gamma rays of hope are sent into your body.
You are injected with the liquid gold of remission.
Your family embraces you with their love and support.
Friends and strangers alike pray on your behalf.

This is God's miracle team.

THE PASSING*

The world has lost a wife, a mother, a teacher, a friend.
Oh the countless lives she has touched.
She loved her family with a Mother's heart and hand.
She earned the adoration of the youth
And the admiration of her peers.

She enriched the lives of her friends by sharing herself.
The world has lost a warrior.
Her armor was the passion she had for life.
She defied science.

She was fearless with the torturous treatments.
Although her body bore the scars of battle,
Her soul, her heart and her spirit remained unmarked.
She embraced life, making each day a celebration.
She was the ultimate teacher of life.

Have we learned to celebrate each day?
She has passed the torch from the here and now
To life eternal.

This is not a sunset but a sunrise.
The pain is gone. Her spirit soars.
All that is left is our sorrow.
The only regret being time…
More time to be a wife, a mother, a teacher, a friend.

Written in memory of Barbara Minney and Vi Bender

CHEMOTHERAPY

Chemotherapy is ex-lax for your hair,
A reason for a nap,
An answer to a bad hair day.

Chemotherapy is little pac-men in your veins
Eating bad things,
The reason why hats were invented.

Is this why your spouse has more time in the bathroom?
Chemotherapy gives you the Aunt Jemima style
When you wear a scarf,
Bonds you emotionally with mannequins,
Sends you to your second infant look prematurely.

Chemotherapy saves you money
On shampoo, conditioner, and hairspray,
Ends your worries about fashionable hair styles,
Takes you out of the gossip circle at your salon.

Chemotherapy provides you the
The alien look for Halloween, makes you
An alien in your own body –
Aaaaaah, you are an alien.

BACK TO THE VAMPIRE ROOM

It is Transylvania in Pennsylvania.
You are led down a hall into a central room.
"It is time to test your blood,"
Pretty and red.

Their fangs come out and they pierce your veins.
You give them the finger and they take that too.
The tubes are filled, the computer is fed
And the numbers are tabulated.

They smile at the thought of blood competition.
Blood is their world.
They read your printout.
"This blood is good."
"No, this blood is great."
Three cheers for the best vampires ever.

JOHN & MARSHA

Here we are, sitting in a circle of chairs –
A circle of hope.
We are all reading magazines – nameless faces.
Everyday the same time, the same thing.

Finally the silence is broken – John & Marsha meet.
"John, John, John, Marsha, Marsha, Marsha."
Does anyone remember that record?

We share more than hands on a clock,
We share the love of children,
We become partners as we walk the hall side by side.
We are wed, not in love, but by
A shared struggle at 2:45.

We exchange stories, laughter, and hot chocolate.
We will soon part – will we meet again?
I feel certain, we are both survivors of the now
With the promise of eternal salvation.

Thank you John, my friend.
I smile and think of the time we'll meet again.

MY DOCTORS

Talk about diversity – this is great news!
I have a lady surgeon;
This alone takes strength in so many ways.
We call her "Dr. J" because
No one can really pronounce her name.

I have an oncologist – just think, another lady,
You've come along way baby.
She appears in her "plain dress"
Of the Amish-Mennonite culture.
Thank God she has more
Than an eighth-grade education.

My radiologist is from India,
Very gifted, factual and a straight-faced professional.
Concerned with a few bald spots on my head when,
Wait – soon I'll be bald just like him.

Then there is me – another funny story,
Because smiling takes away the tears.
We are quite a team.

So here's to you my doctors:
You're OK Dr. "J"
You're not a pain Dr. Kane.
You "sing your story" Dr. Sinapuri,
The story and glory of healing.

Now you must receive my gift of laughter,
That might just be the best medicine yet.

TECHNICIANS OF LIFE

The orders are given,
The simulation is complete.
The next round of warriors
In pink and blue gowns of armor
Descends into the holding room ready for battle.

They are distant nameless faces,
Mostly marked body parts.
As words are shared something happens,
The unknown becomes the known, faces have names.

It is a lot easier without emotions,
When you deal with files and Polaroid pictures.
You must now provide the healing touch,
The calming voice, and the radiation of hope.

For a brief time you are emotionally involved.
How do you deal with the multitudes
Drawing your strength and energy?

The patients move in and out –
But what happens to them?
Do you dare read the obituaries?
How many return to give thanks
For cured bodies and renewed spirits?

You help so many to be survivors,
But who helps you survive
When there is always another hand to hold?

GOOD-BYE

There is a certain comfort in routine.
You feel safe with the daily radiation treatments.
Cancer wouldn't dare progress
With so many doctors, nurses and technicians
Observing and documenting any changes.

They won't let anything happen to you
Under their watch.
You easily adjust your schedule
To revolve around your treatment time.
The car arrives at its space
Almost like it had automatic pilot.

The days have gone by so quickly.
It is so hard to say good-bye
Especially to your personal caregivers, your friends.
For a part of a year, at a specific time,
The people within these walls have become family,
A family fighting a common enemy.

Then your treatments are finished – radiation complete.
You must now walk out the door
To continue your battle alone,
Leaving your team behind.
It's a little sad. It's a little scary.

The very thing you were so afraid you couldn't endure
Is the very thing you are afraid to let go of.
It is so very hard to say good-bye.

Who will fill my time at 2:45?
Who will ask me how I am – with a smile?
Who will be concerned about my weekend plans?
Who will help me fight the fight?
It is tough to walk in and even tougher to walk out.

TEN-CENT NOVEL

My life reads like a ten-cent novel
Purchased in your local discount store.
It's not filled with drinking and sex, just
Chapters of life,
Ones the world might find a bore.

The first chapter is my years as a youth.
My parents adored me, I could do no wrong.
We played hopscotch, ran races
And were just kids all day long.

My parents gave me everything
That they could possibly give.
I owned a horse, played tennis and golf,
It was a great life to live.

I had many friends to have fun with
During the middle chapters of life.
I attended college, played sports, went to parties
All with very little strife.

After school I went to work
And met my husband of today.
We bought a farm, raised two wonderful girls,
For which I'm thankful each time I pray.

Every book must have a tear-jerky chapter
Or it just wouldn't seem true.
It's when they found cancer in my body
The way it changed my life, I hadn't a clue.

I've met numerous doctors,
As they all try to find a cure.
I've had tests and procedures,
Too many to endure.

It is God who has helped me the most,
Lifted me from the valley that I was in.
He has taught me to pray, face my fears,
And put all my trust in Him.

So the chapters of my life continue
And will never end,
For I have the promise of eternal life, faith,
And the love of family and friends.

YOU ARE CORDIALLY INVITED

You are cordially invited to:

A celebration of my birth – my rebirth,
My baptism into the world of believers,
My wedding with Christ – my first love,
My funeral – a celebration of my earthly time
And my send off to life eternal,
Given in honor of any believer.

When: now and forever
Where: right here or whereever
Time: now or whenever

Please RSVP: now not never

HOW DO I SEE THE WORLD?

Sometimes I need to magnify the good,
So I wear reading glasses.
I wear bifocals, the half-and-half vision,
So I can see both near and far,
Kind of like the past, present and future.

Sometimes I want to be blind
To all I have to go through.
Off come the glasses.

I wear glasses with rims so I have tunnel vision,
And see only what is ahead.

Rimless glasses are weightless,
And lighten the burdens of life.

Contacts offer a new world, a new look, a new outlook.
Tears don't smudge on contacts like glasses.

Glasses and contacts really help you
Focus on your problems,
And help you see the solutions more clearly.
Who would have lasik surgery and miss all this?

FINAL DESTINATION

The plane was filled to capacity.
The pilot announced
We were descending to Orlando Airport,
The final destination for all the passengers.

Orlando – paradise for kids and grown-ups alike.
It made me stop and think.
How many on this flight would find
Their final destination with God in heaven?

I look around the airport at the multitudes of tourists.
Are they content in the magic kingdom of fantasy fun,
Artificial existence, temporary happiness?
Time was spent on the many plans,
Money saved in anticipation
Of perfect days and fun in the sun.

Have these people given the same amount of time
To think about their salvation?
Do they fold their hands, bow their heads
And give thanks for their nourishment?
Do they ever thank God for His blessings,
His grace and His love?

All they have to do is ask and believe.
The magic kingdom can become their life
Each and every day and forever.
They can wish upon a star and realize
Dreams do come true because of God.

I think about all these people.
Are they on the right flight
To arrive at their "final destination"?

They need to put their lives in the Pilot's capable hands
Because He knows so much more of what is ahead.
There maybe some turbulence during the ride,
And you might have to fasten the seat belt but
You will arrive safely
If you just let God be the pilot in your life.
Let God take the controls
That determine your "final destination."

MY

My hero, my lover, my best friend, my confidant,
My encourager, my cheerleader, my counselor,
My hand holder, my shoulder to cry on,
My provider, my foot warmer, my playmate,
My dance partner, my funny bone,
My reason for living…
My husband.

EARTHLY ANGEL

Special people come into our lives,
And we are so better for having known them.
One such person was my student
Who later became an irreplaceable friend.

She has a nonstop smile. She would befriend
Anyone and everyone.
She has a heart of gold. She has a deep love for God.
She has taught me to always look on the bright side,
That there is no such thing as self-pity,
That it takes time to be a friend.

She can run like the wind and fly like a bird
While never leaving her wheelchair.
She is a gift from heaven for she truly is
My earthly angel.

THE WONDERS OF WATER

Oh the wonders of water.
Could it be God's daily baptismal, anointing of hope,
His reminder our sins can be washed away?

Water refreshes the body and soul in the morning,
And at night it soothes the daily pain of life.
Water quenches our thirst
With only good and lasting effects.

Oh how water refreshes and filters the earth's air
With its fragrant, beautifying rain,
Giving life to God's creations.

Think of the strength one receives with a daily swim.
You are weightless, submerged in a world
Without pain or fears.

Then there is the softening of the skin
That holds the scars of living.
The whirlpool kneads the muscles of stress.
Worries are washed away.

The water beating out of the shower head
Seems to clear the mind for therapeutic thinking.
The nearness of water
Seems to bring out the greatness in man.

God reveals his creativity,
Offering these gifts to mankind
In the power of the waterfall,
The miracle of the tides,
The rhythm of the waves,
The peacefulness of the lake,
The tranquility of the brook,
The soothing sound of the fountain,
And the gift of tears:
Tears that can help open and heal a hurting heart,
Tears that refresh the soul.

Thank you God for this great gift,
For we were not meant to survive in the desert.

THE APPOINTMENT

Anxiety, high blood pressure, cold hands,
Fake smiles, frustration, the dreaded scale,
Nervous laughter, questions, doubts, fears,
More tests, pricked fingers, pricked veins.

Isn't it ironic? They are on my side,
Fighting for me!
Outside of these walls, I'm sure we would be friends.

HERE WE GO AGAIN

I wonder how doctors react when they are patients.
Do they know what it is like to go through
The multitude of tests they prescribe?
Tests that wear you out
Emotionally more than physically.

It is tough to stay up day after day, test after test.
You read your "fear nots" in the Bible.
You breathe deeply to take away the stress.

Then your name is called.
Here we go again – more tests.

BIONIC BREASTS

Oh the life of breasts.

They have been clothed in undershirts,
Then training bras.
They have been made to look bigger
With handkerchiefs and padded cups.
They have been lifted and separated.
We've even crossed our hearts.

They have been flattened for athletics.
They have been cuddled in passion.
They have been a source of nourishment for babies.
They have acted as a pillow in a comforting hug.
They have been photographed, not for Playboy,
But as a medical documentation.

They have had perky years and years they hang low.
They even have names.
They have been a pincushion for needles.
They have been mashed in mammography,
Smashed with ultrasound,
And slashed in surgery.

The good news is they are still here.
They are priceless.
The insurance company, at the very least,
Thinks they should be bionic.

HEARING AID

Was God always talking to me and I just didn't hear?
I never was a good listener.
I was never on the right station,
And I know the volume was never turned up.

Then I was reborn and so were my senses.
God has my attention.
His music is now heard.
It is so inspirational and uplifting.

Daily I hear his words of encouragement.
I see my friends, his angels, surrounding me with love.
I feel his comforting arms.
God is my hearing aid
And He has brought all my senses back to life.

Please keep calling me, Lord, just keep calling,
And I will listen.

ANOTHER PHONE CALL
(January 14, 2005)

Early in the morning the telephone rang.
It was my oncologist I saw yesterday, Dr. Joan Kane.

My husband talked but I could tell by his eyes,
I didn't want to hear her and I was about to cry.

The news he heard he didn't want to deliver:
I needed more blood work, something could be wrong
with my liver.

I closed my eyes and I said a prayer,
"Please God. Please God, Please not there."

I shed a few tears,
This is the one place I feared.

We embrace, my husband who is my best friend,
He said we'll get through this, it cannot be the end.

A thought crossed my mind and I shot him a look,
I need to get busy and complete this book.

I think this is God's purpose why I live cancer's hell,
So I can help others through it with the poetry and the
story I tell.

In one year I've had all treatments available to this date,
All prescribed by doctors who in the cancer field are
top rate.

I've had hormones and surgery, radiation and
chemotherapy drugs,
All in an attempt to end the invasion of the cancer
thugs.

The treatments are soon complete,
I feel this is a disease I can defeat.

This phone call truly was a blow to my mind,
If it is spreading again, what else would they find?

Off we go to give blood for more tests,
All I really want is to just give it all a rest.

They would call with the results by the end of the day,
The phone rang as promised, HURRAY, I'm OK.

DON'T FEEL SORRY FOR ME

"There she is."
"Did you know?"
"I feel so badly."
"What about her family?"
"Should we say anything?"
"I just feel so sorry for her."

Sorry for me – are you kidding?
I'm the luckiest person on earth.
I have the greatest life.
In good times and bad I have
The love of a wonderful family.
I have a soul mate in my husband.
There is joy in our home.
We have the respect of our children.

We surround ourselves with true and caring friends.
I have a heart relationship with God.
He has replaced my fears with a wonderful promise.
We are content – we have what we want
And we want what we have – nothing more.

Birth and death are a given.
It is what we do in between that is up to us.
I choose to give it my all, enjoying each day,
Each hour, and every breath.

I laugh a lot and I smile when I think of what I have.
So, feel sorry for me?
Never – I have it all and then some.

FRIDAY

As a parent we think we know what love is.
We are consumed with feelings for our children.
Our every thought, our very being
From the time of their birth
Revolves around their existence and their welfare.

Then we think of the magnitude of God's love
And there is no comparison.
For he sacrificed his only son Jesus for our salvation,
For us yesterday, today and forever.

This happened some two thousand years ago.
Jesus was tortured and died a horrible death.
The impact of that day is still felt,
Tears still flow with grief.

The good news is we know the rest of the story,
The joy of the resurrection.
We thank you God for loving us so very much,
And for your mercy and grace. We exalt your name.
For believers this is not only a "Good Friday,"
It is a "Great Friday" – Alleluia!

TAKE THE TIME

What about this fast-paced life we live in?
Time is our most important natural resource.
We seem to have forgotten what is important.

More is better.
Bigger is better.
Faster is better.
Isn't it time to slow down?

Maybe now is the time
To not only smell the roses but to plant a garden.
We need to give meaningful time
To the people in our lives, the people we love.
Show you care.

Now is the time to…
Realize the importance of writing
A letter instead of sending an e-mail.
Visit face to face, don't just leave
A message on a machine.
Put on an apron and cook
A four-course meal instead of serving fast food.
Read to each other instead of watching television.

Take time to pray together.
God can hear two voices better than one.
Realize a warm hug and a loving kiss
Are worth more than diamonds.
Light a candle instead of turning on a light.
Remember it is more important
To give "time" than material gifts.

Give, don't always take.
Take time to hold hands,
It is amazing how hearts connect.

Read the book instead of watching the movie version.
Take a walk and talk instead of driving the car.
Look into someone's eyes, you can hear so much better.
Spend time with your kids instead of all your meetings.
You'll never regret it.

Life is just too short so take the time
To live, love and laugh,
And always "Be nice."

REMEMBERING

Remembering the brick wall in the back of the building.
Remembering the blast of heat in the entrance way,
Like the heat of radiation.

Remembering the faces, new faces terrorized by cancer,
Looking down at magazines, no one wanting to be here.
Remembering the sweet hot chocolate as you wait,
The bonus.

Remembering the pink and blue gowns,
They seem smaller this time.
Remembering the machine – ready, aim, fire –
I say the Lord's Prayer.

Remembering it only takes a few minutes,
But what really happens to the cells?
Remembering you are to relax and breathe normally,

What is normal now?

Remembering all the familiar faces so happy to see you,
But so sorry you are here!
Here we go again – remembering.

OUR SINS ARE TAKEN AWAY

Oh the effects of sins.
They truly cripple the mind and body.
There is devastating depression, sadness,
Loneliness and despair.
There is the debilitating fear of life itself
And the fear of death.

When Jesus died on the cross, he bled to cleanse us,
To free us and to deliver us from all evil.
His blood released us from the bondage of sin.
He broke the chains that held us in wrongful living.

We can have this freedom for the asking.
Confess and believe and you will be saved.
Come "into me" not just "unto me" for true peace.
Life's chaos is put to order through faith.

Each and every day we have power
Because of Jesus' resurrection.
Jesus gives us a reason to live and a reason to die.

SURVIVORS

How many of us walking this earth
Have faced the cancer foe?

Oh the battles we have fought.
The tests we have endured.
The emotional and physical scars we bear.
We are changed people.

We do not have the brand "C" on our foreheads,
But we know who we are.
We wear the pink ribbon of hope.
We fund-raise to fight the disease.

We give guidance to the rookies.
We read and we research.
We write to help ourselves and others.

We are fighters.
We are friends.
We are, in a sense, heroes of life.

THE ROLLER COASTER

Why do we always have to fight?
Each day we go to battle against cancer.
The problem is the battle is within our body.
You have to fight yourself.

It is a true love-hate relationship.
You go through the highs and lows,
A roller coaster of emotions.

You face the fears of tests.
You are paralyzed until your results are known.
Your imagination goes wild as you wait.

What is this pain?
Have the cells spread?
Is it just a headache?
Is this the end?

Cancer is like a ride on a roller coaster.
It is so difficult to go uphill.
It is a very slow mechanical process.
It is much easier and faster
To free fall down into depression.

There are so many peaks and valleys.
We go around and around.
Will we ever get off this ride?

As a child it would be great fun
To ride a roller coaster forever.
As an adult with cancer – it needs to stop.

THE PRIZE FIGHTER

It is almost a knock-out punch in the first round.
You gasp for air, your head is swirling,
Your family watches in stunned silence.
You are diagnosed with cancer.

You push yourself up off the mat
Before the count is over.
You raise your fists for your fight has just begun.
You strike surgically but your opponent still stands.
Second round over.

Your coach suggests you circle your foe,
Taking slow steps with chemotherapy.
He counters with some jabs of his own –
Fatigue, nausea and depression.

Then he lands a real blow and knocks
Your hair clean off.
The bell rings. Third round complete.
You've lost some ground.

You are excited in the fourth.
You connect with a succession of spiritual hits.
God smiles in your corner.
Each time you strike back
Your friends in the audience cheer wildly.
You easily took the last round.

In the fifth you connect with hormones,
Vitamins, and bone strengtheners.
Your opponent still stands.

The sixth begins. Your coach is sure you can take him.
You come out with rapid blows of radiation,
10 - 20 - 30 hits!
All this exertion zaps your strength and energy.
He connects squarely leaving a painful red mark.
You shake it off.
You know he is losing his footing.
He is definitely weakening.
You sense you can win this fight.
Your adrenaline takes over.
You want to end it now
But the battle continues and continues.
But as long as it continues there is always
The hope of victory.

Your coach never leaves your corner,
Always giving instruction,
Sometimes changing the game plan.
Your loving family and faithful friends
Never leave ringside,
Always cheering, always encouraging.
You feel everyone's support.

But the truth is, you are alone in the ring
With the opponent. How much longer?
Everything is in slow motion.
You are exhausted.
You cannot wait to hear the final bell,
To see whose arm is raised in victory.
…But the fight continues.

ORDINARY

Oh the beauty God has created on this earth.
We go to see the majestic Rocky Mountains,
The power of Niagara Falls.
We visit the glorious and colorful Grand Canyon.
We see the strength and longevity of the redwoods.
God's world is grand and you need grand.

Then one day cancer is introduced
Into your life with its power.
How you change.
You no longer need the extraordinary,
The ordinary is enough.

When once you needed fields of flowers,
You now have the same feelings with just one blossom.
You hear the song of a single bird.
You don't worry about wrinkles, you cherish them.

You even look forward to growing older.
You love walking, looking at the colors,
Taking in nature.
You don't always have to compete
Or get better, just doing is enough.

Your life truly changes.
You have different priorities.
You become content with less.
Can cancer make you a better or a happier person?
Maybe, just maybe.

CONNECT

Hugs connect hearts.
Laughter connects spirits.
Prayers connect souls.
This is life.
This is God's hope for us.
This is what makes us beautiful.
This is what counts.
This is how we connect.

HOPE

Hope is a little word with infinite power.
Hope is strong and bold and beautiful.
Hope enables us and dares us to believe
That all will work out, all is OK.

Hope is an empty vessel only we can fill.
Hope makes life bearable and
Where there is life there can always be hope.
Hope is…

A FOREVER BOND

There is a special bond between mothers and daughters.
There is a connection, a connection of hearts and souls.
As a child we are unaware because our needs are met,
But we hold hands.

As we grow older so do our feelings grow.
We share wisdom, we listen, we learn, we spend time.
Our mother-daughter connection is a deep love.

If we are very lucky, God gives us special people –
Chosen mothers –
To help us journey through life.

Birth isn't even significant for this relationship.
We meet later,
We choose each other,
We help each other,
We worry about each other and we pray for each other.
We are deeply blessed by our relationship.

Sometimes the bond created is even stronger,
When strangers become mothers and daughters.
This chosen bond is forever.

THE SECRET OF LIFE

Learning from others leads to intelligence.
Listening to others takes intelligence.

It takes wisdom and deep insight to know yourself.
To learn, you need strength in mind and body.

To understand one's self is a never-ending process.
Be content with what you have, this leads to happiness.

If your center is happy and good,
You understand what you lose in death
And you better appreciate life.

To really live you must die first.
If you pass this understanding to others,
You live forever.

A MOTHER'S HEART

A mother's heart is so full of love.
When their children hurt, a mother's heart breaks.
Her heart cries real tears of sadness.
Her heart breaks wanting to take away the pain.
But somehow a mother's heart keeps beating
The healing rhythm of life.

PRAYER

You must learn to talk to your God,
Have a holy conversation.
Open your heart.
Open your hurts.
Open your mind.

And you must listen for your answers.
Hear the voice of the Lord.
Prayer is your dialog.
June 28th, they found cancer in my right breast.

HOW DO I REALLY FEEL?

I feel quiet, I feel sad.
I feel drained, I feel let down.
I feel disappointed, I feel lifeless.
I feel my hopes and dreams
Are buried under anxieties and fears.

I feel I've let everyone down.
Why can't I get better?
Why aren't the treatments working?
Were all those prayers worthless?
Were my prayers even heard?

I feel now my faith is being tested.
I still feel so close to God.
Please listen.
Please don't let me down.

LIVE EACH DAY

No one leaves this earth alive.
What would we be like if we lived each day
As if death were in the near future?

Would we make the most of every moment?
Would we live each day positively?
Would we choose to create memorable experiences?
Would we spend quality time with our loved ones?
Would we write a "to do" list and do them?

Could we just stop worrying about the future,
About work, about money,
And most importantly about our family?
Could we end frustration, anxiety, and jealousy?

We need to live each moment for love,
Laughter and happiness,
And togetherness with our God and family and friends.

The world is not dark.
We must open our eyes and see the light.
We must learn to live each day as if it were our last.

FILL ME

Fill my lungs with air to sing your praises.
Fill my heart with love to share your love for mankind.
Open my eyes to your beauty so I can see and share
The beauty of your created world.
Fill my soul with your spirit so I can be
A bright light in your world.
Fill me, dear Lord. Fill me not half way but fully.

WRITE

The first thing you must always remember
Is you will always forget.
What seems vitally important today
Will someday be a forgotten experience or thought.

So write about your activities.
Document the facts.
Tell your story.
Express your feelings.

One small event can shape a person
Or ignite change in the world.
Don't keep it inside. Share with others.

We are both teachers and students
Because of the written word.
Everyone should write.

A FLOWER – A LIFE

Life is like a flower.
We start as a bulb, small and wrapped
And protected from the world,
Just like we are in our mother's womb.

We slowly sprout and finally grow
Bursting through the earth's crust.
We flourish taking in nourishment and water
And receiving God's miraculous sunlight.

We develop as individuals like the bud forming.
The flower breaks out and shows its petals to the world
With all the splendid color and beauty.

That is our goal, to lift our faces to the heavens,
Take direction
And make the world a better place for all.

We are strong and bold and bright,
But just as the flower, we are bound to fade
And one day we will both be a memory.

But that is what life is,
A series of special moments
Just like a bouquet given in love.

TRUE LOVE

Love is the rapid beating of the heart.
It is the longing to be with that one special person.
It is an exchange of vows before God.
Love is a promise made and kept forever.
It is a kiss and a special touch.

But true love is so much more.
True love means staying and supporting
Through the hard times and the tears.
It means loving the imperfections and the scars
When beauty is only a memory.

True love is walking side by side holding hands tightly
When the road is rough
And you don't know what lies ahead.
True love leaps any obstacle in tandem and with grace.
True love is deep and forever.

LOVE IS

Love isn't the size and sparkle
Of the diamond on your finger:
It is the twinkle of love in your eyes.

Love isn't the square footage of the home you live in:
It is the size and passion in your heart.

Love isn't handing over gifts for special occasions:
It is walking together every day hand in hand.

Love isn't giving the weekly paycheck:
It is giving the daily support and understanding.

Love is from within, given freely.
Love is and should always be.

FACE YOUR FEARS

Fear is a universal experience.
It is a part of being alive.
Fear can be a small hurdle to overcome
Or it can totally paralyze a person.
Fear can be bigger than life itself.

You must let your fears be known,
Because God knows them already.
They cannot be hidden under a blanket of denial.
They cannot be masked by smiles.

Fears can be conquered but will never be totally erased,
Just faded by faith.
You must face your fears head on,
Or fears will overwhelm you into a weakened state
Of helplessness or passiveness.

You must constantly unveil your feeling
To yourself first and to the Lord.
You must admit, confess, release and move on.

And then you can relax,
Because of your openness and your faith,
Faith that your fears have been met.

MY FRIENDS, MY QUILTS

My friends are like the quilts in my home.
Some I see every day and others
Are folded and tucked in drawers,
Only to be brought out on special occasions.
In my heart, all are cherished.

My quilts are all sizes.
There are small potholders, place mats and pillows.
I have medium framed decorations
And larger quilts for warmth.
New quilts and antique creations
Grace my walls and beds.

Each one is unique, as are my friends,
But all are stitched with threads of love.
There is the "Lone Star,"
The "Diamond in the Square,"
"Grandma's Flower Garden" and of course,
The "Crazy Quilt."

My dear friends, you are the diamonds,
The sunshine, and the flowers of my life.
You crazy ones make me laugh.
Thank you for the beauty and the color you give to me
Each and every day.
You are all treasured just like my quilts.

YOU ARE YOU

Sometimes it is hard to be yourself.
It is hard to look in the mirror
And see the imperfections.
It is hard to look into your soul
And see the needed changes.
It is hard to hear your heart and know what is missing.

Sometimes it is hard to be you,
But it is easier than being someone else.
Who you are is a given, no trade ins.
You are you, for better or worse.
So look into that mirror and smile.

THE RHYTHM OF LIFE

There is a rhythm to life.
We walk and talk in a cadence.
Our hearts beat rhythmically.
We breathe in and we breathe out.
We are surrounded by the ebb and flow
Of the world and its objects.

There is the tick, tock of the clock.
We hear the beat of music.
We see dancers' feet move in harmony.
The ocean waves and tides have a predictable pattern.
The seasons change with the calendar.

We know there are always 24 hours in each day
And seven days in each week.
We expect the birth of the baby
And accept the death of the aged.
There is peace when life's rhythm is undisturbed.

But we also know there are storms and tragedies
That disrupt the peaceful rhythm of life.
These are unpredictable changes
In our once predictable world.
Changes of jobs, homes, family situations, illness
And most painfully,
The untimely death of a loved one.
Our once peaceful existence is in turmoil.

It is difficult, but now is the time
To trust God and accept the grace he offers,
To help us accept the changes life brings.
In time, He will return the rhythm of life.

NIGHTTIME

Why is the nighttime so difficult?
Is it because we are alone in the dark
With only our thoughts?
For most, quiet is scary.

At night we cannot escape the stillness.
Everything is scarier at night.
Problems are blown out of proportion.
You become distraught with fears.

The "what if's," the "should have's" and the "why's"
Take over.
The promise of a new day seems light years away.
Your eyes are wide open but you don't see a thing,
Not even the time on the clock.

You don't have answers to your questions, just
More questions.
Your thoughts move in the fast forward mode.
Your mind is like a whirlwind.
You listen for anything, your own breathing,
The sounds of the house.

Why can't your body just give into sleep?
Finally your eyes close and the alarm rings.
It is morning.

All you want to do is sleep.

GET UP AND WALK

Do not lie down on a mat of excuses.
Do not set up camp
With tents of sadness, depression or anxiety.
Tents that are woven out of threads
Of fear, anger and bitterness.

You can bury your head in a pillow of denial.
You can close your eyes to the world
Seeing only black, seeing nothing.

God asks us to get up and walk out of our black hole.
He has given us the grace and the courage to change.
He has given us the strength to get up and walk.

It is our choice.
Don't let the weight of the world hold you down.
Get up and walk now.

I WILL NOT DIE NOW

I will not die now because…

My calendar is full of activities.
I just don't have time.
I really cannot fit it into my schedule.
I'm taking on new jobs
And the old ones are not finished.
I'm still needed as a mother and wife,
And I'm looking forward someday to being a grandma.
There are years of pictures to be put in albums.
I need to finish decorating the house.
I have books to read and movies to see,
Golf courses to play.
I have lunch dates with friends.
There are places I want to visit.
I want time to grow old with my husband,
Side by side and hand in hand.
I want to watch my kids experience life.

Die??? Not now.
I just have way too much to do.
Maybe later.

MY GREAT ESCAPE

Just for a short time I am the leading lady
In the Hollywood movie.
I am the star of the television show.
I am the heroine in the romance novel.

I am the Olympic athlete winning the gold medal.
I am a singer in a musical.
I am the eagle soaring in the sky.
When things get difficult,
My mind can take me to a different place.

I am whatever and wherever my imagination takes me.
For an instant, in my thoughts
I can live in a different world.
It is my great escape.
Sometimes, it is my only escape.

SUNDAY

Sunday brings people together.

It is a gathering of believers who share a love of God.
It is a day to fill up at God's gas station.
It is a day to have your spirit renewed.
A day to receive the cathedral light,
The true light, God's enlightenment.
You are offered a promise of a new life,
A life where you receive rest and peace,
Through the security of salvation.

Sunday is the listening of the word, God's word.
It is the singing of God's praises.
Sunday is a gathering of people
Who listen to your prayer requests to God.

These people help bear your burdens.
It is the sharing of tears and joys.
It is the release of troubled hearts.
We are asked to lay our fears
At the foot of the cross and be healed.

Sunday is a day to be filled with the trust of the Lord.
It is a day of sun, of light, of joy, of true peace.
Sunday we renew our love vows with God
And strengthen our faith,
A faith that helps us live
The rest of the days of the week.

LOVE LETTER TO GOD

You are the complete Father,
The perfect Husband,
And the ultimate Friend.

You are my All in All.
You are all I need to live.
You get me through each day, in happiness or sorrow.

You listen whenever I speak.
You are the answer to every question
And every problem.

You are the reason for our joys.
I give You my love and my thanks.
I give You me.

WRONG TURN

How easily I get distracted from
My purpose I once saw so clearly.
I take on new challenges and become totally consumed.

All the paths I've previously trodden
Have become covered with weeds,
As I now walk in a tunnel along a one way road.

My thoughts, my energy and my time
Are directed toward one goal.
Is this what I'm to do?

Is this the right road on my life's map,
Or have I made a wrong turn?
There is a price.
There is a sacrifice.
There arc consequences.

SAY THE WORD

Say the word "cancer."
Acknowledge it for what it is.
It is no longer a death sentence.
Cancer is a disease,
One that can be controlled and cured.

When you speak the word "cancer"
You diminish its power.
You lessen the fears.
You take control and with this control comes strength,
The strength you need to live life to the fullest.

MY NEW BEST FRIENDS

Today I'm introduced to twin bags hanging on a pole.
Today I meet taxol and carboplatin,
My new best friends.
I'm thankful, not fearful,
That they, the chemotherapy drugs, are in my life.

I accept their liquid gold of healing,
Dripping slowly into my systems.
They are the warriors
Waging war on my overactive cells.

I envision them as "pac-men" racing around my veins.
Gobbling and devouring all that is bad.
When you are introduced to new things in your life
There are always changes.

Yes, there will be changes. I accept them with grace.
But I'm grateful for these new friends.
They are my life supporters, my life lengtheners.
Welcome to my world.

MY DANCE PARTNER

My pole is loaded with bags.
I'm plugged into the wall.
We are connected in so many ways.
The fluid drips into my veins through long plastic tubes.
I drink and drink and drink.

The liquids go in and the liquids go out.
My partner and I dance to the bathroom.
I'm dizzy and my pole has a mind of its own.
What a combination.

I follow my partner that has four left feet.
He pirouettes but I refuse to spin.
I want to go left and he wants to go right.
I hang on as we zigzag across the room
All tangled up in tubes, trying not to hit anyone.

I laugh as we finally reach our destination, a bathroom.
On the way back I decide to take the lead,
And we waltz through the room without missing a beat.

I get untangled, plugged in
And situated in my comfy chair.
Fifteen minutes later my song plays
And we dance again.

TRUE COMPETITOR

Are we all born to compete?
Is there a gene in us
That guides and fires us up to be the best?

We compete in school for better grades.
We compete on athletic playing fields to be the victor.
We compete in the work force
For better jobs and higher pay.

We lift weights to become stronger.
We run to get lighter, faster and to be in better shape.
We want to look good and feel good,
To be competitive in a competitive world.
We want to win.

But there are always setbacks, injury and disease,
Yes disease, the would-be could-be end-all.
When disease hits, you need
To call on that competitive gene,
For the fight has begun, the competition for life itself.

You can give in and give up,
Or let the competitive juices flow.
I say, "Bring it on."

I'm strong in mind, body and soul.
I'm a true competitor - a gladiator.
Let the fight begin without commercial breaks.

BRING IT ON

You little cancer cells.
You cannot beat me.
I'm big and strong and full of faith.
Faith that replaces all fears
And gives me immeasurable strength.

So bring it on, give me your best shot.
No matter how small or big you become I will prevail,
For you'll never be strong enough
To touch my heart or soul.

DID I EVER TELL YOU*

Did I ever tell you when you were born
That I was scared beyond words?
I was a Mother without any knowledge,
Any experience or any credentials.

You cried and I cried.

You were born into a world that was foreign to me.
Each hour, each day, each year we grew together.
The cries of want and need
Turned into words of communication that bond hearts.
The fears transformed into deep and comforting love
Needed to survive each day.

We walk together, side by side,
Hand in hand, learning from each other.
Did I ever tell you that you changed my life forever?

You are my reason to live.
You are my greatest gift
And the greatest gift I could give the world.

Written for Kimberlee on her birthday

BORN AGAIN*

My eyes were closed but I could hear
The most precious of words, "a little girl."
Thank you God, you answered my prayers.

I held you tightly never wanting you to grow.
Despite my efforts you broke out,
Leaving your footprints on every heart you touch.

While in my arms a deep, loving bond developed.
We are so much more than genetics.
As you grew we learned from each other.

We helped and guided each other.
We protected each other.
We always loved each other.

You ran like the wind,
Excelling in everything you attempted.
You exemplified the Olympian spirit every day.

Looking deeper than the physical
Is the heart bond that developed, our real connection.
I know your hurts. I triumph with your successes.

We struggle together as you aim for the stars,
Always striving for the highest,
Always pushing to the limits.

We are so much the same as if there was a rebirth.
We are connected in spirit. Our souls are one.
I know, for our hearts beat in the same rhythm.

* *Written for Melissa*

FULL TIME JOB

I must apologize to the world.
God has a full time job sitting on my shoulder.

The Bible says God knows
The number of hairs on our heads.
With me He has to count and recount and count again,
Continually.

I'm truly sorry. Right now He doesn't have time
To answer other's prayers.
He is too busy with me.

Three weeks, two days and four hours
After my first chemotherapy, it started!
My hair was thinning.

In the beginning it wasn't much but in a week
God had his hands full.
And so did I, hands full of hair.

At the very least God needs a calculator
To keep count as I continually shed hair.
God has a full time job counting the hairs on my head.
Soon He'll be retired because
The clippers are coming out.

Don't worry God, I still need you!

ROUND AND SMOOTH

A ping pong ball, a "Q" tip, a nectarine,
An orange, a bowling ball, my head.
Smooth and round.
Oh the joys of chemotherapy.
It is definitely a no hair day.

WHAT MAKES US BEAUTIFUL

Our society equates beauty with appearance.
We judge not on what's on the inside
But with what we see on the outside.

We first see body shape and hairstyle.
We strive for the perfect figure,
A wrinkle-free face, eliminating the sign of age.

And we want soft, thick, beautifully colored,
Flowing locks of hair.
Billions are spent on cosmetics and hair products.
Our hairdresser becomes our best friend.
Life is good. We are beautiful to the eye,
A real glamour girl.

Wham! Cancer hits
And treatments dull your complexion, add pounds,
And chemotherapy thins your hair
Until finally you are bald.
But bald is beautiful too.

Now is the time to shine.
Don't cower and hide.
Let your personality illuminate the world.
Let your inner beauty burst open like a flower,
Like fireworks –
You can light the darkness.

You show the world what's really beautiful.
So "you go girl" and dance and be merry.

MY MOTHER

I don't remember when you weren't plagued by cancer.
You were the first soldier I ever knew,
Going to battle every day,
Against an enemy in their own body.

I wish I had asked you about this fight.
I don't remember tears. You should have cried.
I don't remember anger.
You had every reason to be raging mad.

I don't remember any complaining
Although you could have moaned profusely.
I wish I had asked you about your heart feelings.

You lived for me. You lived to travel.
You lived to play. You lived hard and life was hard.
I wish we had talked about how you felt
Concerning life and death.

There were radical surgeries, stays in the hospital,
And drugs were developed and tried.
God waved his miraculous hand over you
And for several extra years,
You were OK. I think. I never asked.

I have so many questions that will go unanswered.
So many conversations were never spoken.
I wish I knew more about you.
When I make the final journey, I hope we can talk.

THE WORLD MEETS GABBY

Gabby and I walk out the door together.
She is cute and blond and perky.
Her hair is short with shaggy bangs
And her ends flip up in the back
Making her look a little sassy.

Wherever we walk, strangers smile.
Wherever we go, Gabby demands attention.
We all know people like that.

My friends are all excited to meet Gabby.
They giggle when they are introduced.
Everyone likes her. She is accepted in my circle.

Having her around makes me look younger,
So say my friends.
I hope so because we are truly connected.
Gabby is a part of me, a part of my life.

According to my insurance company,
Gabby is my cranial prosthesis.
To you and me, Gabby is my wig.
We are one hot, old Mama – Gabby and me.

MY HEAD ITCHES

I'm bald, my head itches.
There are red bumps on my scalp from the wig.
My ears look big. My tummy aches. I'm tired.
Sometimes I hurt.

Hurray for chemotherapy.
No complaints.
I'm alive!

THE PHONE CALL

The hour has come. You wait
For the promised phone call from your doctor.
The biopsy report lies on his desk.
You pace as you impatiently wait
For the chime of the phone.

You are unable to sit or even think.
You nervously walk and walk.
Your breathing is shallow and rapid.
Your heart pounds in your chest and ears.

The phone finally rings and you jump in your skin.
You steady your voice.
He speaks his sympathetic words. He is very sorry.

He asks if I am OK.
He asks if I am alone.
He doesn't want me to be by myself.

I'm assured that he'll be a part
Of my medical support team.
You hear the agony in his voice.
You feel sorry for him.

He knows that he has just shattered your world.
You console him.
I'll get through this. I'll be fine. I am a fighter.

I am grateful that he has empathy for his patients.
Caring makes it personal,
Maybe too personal for a doctor with so many patients.
Can he survive?

He quickly becomes my favorite caregiver
Even though he was a giver of sad news.
Even through the phone lines we connect.

Thank you for caring.
Please don't ever change.
Caring is the best medicine he could give.

HAROLD'S LAST DAY

Harold walked through these doors 24 times.
He had needles in his veins 24 times.
He fought the effects of chemotherapy 24 times.
Because of Harold I know the importance
Of the last day.

To celebrate I baked cookies and wrote him a song.
He smiled and expressed his thanks
And kissed me on the cheek in appreciation.
Then he said goodbye to his caregivers.

He walked away from us, away from the people
And poles and IV's full of chemicals.
He slowly walked through the familiar doors
For the last time.
He quietly departed.

I promise myself I will sing
And dance in celebration of my last treatment.
I'll always remember Harold.

HAROLD'S SONG

(after the song "So Long, Farewell" from "The Sound of Music")

So long, farewell to Harold we say adieu.
His 24 rounds of chemo now are through.
Dididididididididididididi

There's times in life that don't seem always fair,
But God and friends and families always there.
Dididididididididididididi

We wish him luck while out the door he'll fly.
The time has come for us to say goodbye.
Goodbye, goodbye goodbye
[group] goodbye.

A TREE

I see a tree standing alone on the horizon.
It is a tree of life starting as a small seed in the ground.
Over the years it grows and flourishes,
Spreading its limbs out to the world,
Like outstretched, loving and embracing arms
Of a Mother.

They are limbs that protect earth's creatures
From the elements of above.
They provide the goodness and coolness of shade,
And become the sifting shields from rain.
I see my life in this tree.

During the growing stages, my purpose on earth
Is just starting to unfold.
Each season of my life, I bloom. The fruits come.
God unveils His gifts, in me, to benefit His world.
Each season, each year, there are so many changes.

The one constant is growth.
I see the tangled branches of a cluttered life,
And the tree weakens.
God eventually prunes the vines,
Restoring strength and giving direction.

The way becomes clearer and I continue to grow.
There is a stage when we all are in full bloom.
You are in your prime. The leaves are countless.
Then the wind of disease prematurely forces the leaves
To take flight and fall.

The scars of life begin to show.
Branches break away and time takes its toll.
The outer bark is rugged and worn
From weather and age.

Is God so much a part of my life
That His initials are carved into
My skin, my heart and my soul?

Our days on earth are numbered,
Just as the leaves on the tree.
One by one they fall to the ground, season after season.

I stand now, somewhere between the years,
No longer a seedling.
I watch as each leaf of my life
Flutters in the peaceful wind,
Wondering when the last leaf will take flight,
And limbs are lifeless,
And the tree and I will be but a memory.

MY LAST DAY OF CHEMOTHERAPHY

I want to jump and click my heels together.
I want to dance. I want to shout. I want to sing.
I want butterflies to be freed. I want doves to fly.
I want balloons to float to heaven,
All giving thanks to God.

I want flowers for everyone.
I want sparklers and fireworks to celebrate my victory.
But I will settle for a kiss from my husband.
We did it together.

CANCER'S ACROSTIC POEM

C an
A ggressive, overactive
N asty, malignant, multiplying
C ells be cured, and
E very life be spared the
R avaging effect of a worthless disease?

THE RAZOR

I've had it.
Too much hair is falling out. It's everywhere.
The time has come to take control.

I call my hairdresser. She had been forewarned.
I'm ready and she is ready too, razor in hand.
She nicely shaves the remaining hair in the back
Leaving the front for last.

She doesn't want me to get upset.
We laugh as I am now officially and totally bald.
I would feel so much better
If she would shave her head too.
There are limits to any friendship.

As we are laughing, in walks my florist
With a single, long stem rose in hand.
The card enclosed reads "Smile, I love you, Rich."

The laughter turns into tears. Everyone is crying.
I feel like the luckiest person on earth.

BIOPSY NOW

You've waited for your mammogram results.
Suspicions.
You've had ultrasounds trying to confirm them.
More suspicions.

They found a small lump, a mere bump in my breast.
Confirm or end suspicions?
Biopsy now or later?
Now, now, now.
With time fears will grow, grow, grow.

You are prepped and numbed
And a small gun is fired into the area.
You hold the technician's comforting hand.
Her presence makes a difference.
Several times it is zapped.
They have their suspicions.

Biopsy complete but it is really just the start.
It's been a long day.

1 in 8 women will have breast cancer in their lifetime.
I'm taking the fall for seven of my closest friends.

FRIENDS

Love travels miles and is always felt.
A cheery phone call. Homemade soup.
A sunshine kind of card.

A loaf of bread. Prayers and more prayers.
An unexpected visit. A hand held.
A prayer shawl knitted with threads of love.

A smile. A comforting hug.
A lunch date. Time spent together.

Shared joys, shared laughter, shared tears.
I love my friends!

CANCER COUPLETS

Cancer is a disease we all seem to fear,
No one is immune, attacking those near and dear.

Before I had cancer I didn't like the color pink,
Now the cure and the color are connected, I think.

One in eight women will have breasts that are affected,
But so many can be survivors the earlier it is detected.

Please know your body and get a regular screening,
That is how you fight the disease giving cancer less
meaning.

When you have cancer you are first sad then mad,
But you learn so much about yourself that it's not all
bad.

There are so many tests and treatments you now must
endure,
But where there is life there is hope and we hope for a
cure.

Although the statistics show cancer is on the rise,
I say, live each day to the fullest, thanking God you are
alive.

LET ME FEEL YOU LORD

Let me feel you Lord.
Send down your sunshine to warm my heart.
Cleanse my soul with your rain.
Let me see your mercy
In the darkness of the night through your stars.

Get my attention with bolts of lightning.
Show me your hope in the rainbow.
Let me feel you with every breath I take.
I want to feel you Lord, everywhere I go.

H WORDS

Harmony, Hope, Health,
Healing, Hands, Hearts,
Happiness, Heaven, Hurray!

HAPPINESS

If you radiate happiness
The world might just catch it,
And we would have an epidemic
Of smiles!

EACH DAY

The day breaks. The sun rises in your world.

Each day is a new beginning, a new chance
To smile,
To laugh,
To choose your path of happiness,
To learn from the yesterdays and,
To focus on the moment and make it positive.

Because soon that moment will be yesterday,
And you are only left the promise of tomorrow.

Living the now positively makes the soul shine,
Sending warmth to the world.

MOVE NOW

The mountain looms ahead.
There is a well worn path around the base.
The mustard seed stands boldly
In front of the ominous rocks.

The mustard seed does not follow the others.
It says to the mountain,
"Move now and let me pass.
You are my fears. You are my doubts.
You are my struggles. You are my anxieties.
You are my sins.
Thanks to God my faith is big enough
To move you out of my life,
To allow me to live in peace and hope and love."

God's miracles never cease.
The walls part. A red carpet is rolled down
The very center of the boulder.
The movement of the rocks sounds like applause

And the mustard seed smiles.
It moves ahead always following God's lead.
With faith as small as a mustard seed
Anything is possible.

All is well.
That is God's promise to us.

TO TELL THE TRUTH

"Hi. It's been so long since I've seen you.
Your hair looks great."

Do I tell her or just say thank you?
That is the million dollar question.
I choose both.
"Thank you but to be honest it is a wig.
I'm back into chemotherapy."

Now it makes me wonder:
If everyone likes the "new do,"
How awful was the real thing?

Maybe I'll keep the wig for the "no" hair days of today,
And the "bad" hair days of the future.

THEY NEVER TOLD ME

They never told me how much my arm would hurt
After breast surgery.
The pain was so intense in an arm that seemed numb.

They never told me my breast would be tender
For years and years.

They never told me how hard it would be
To take a shower or look in the mirror.

They never told me how the chemotherapy
Would change my digestive system,
And that the steroids would keep me up all night.

They never told me how very kind people would be,
Or how close you become with your caregivers.

They never told me I would be reunited with my sisters,
A new closeness would develop.

They never told me my husband and I
Would become inseparable,
And that quality time wasn't important,
Just time together was.

They never told me God would be
My best friend, my savior.

They never told me I could be "well" despite having
Stage four cancer.

They never told me I could be so full
Of happiness and love and thankfulness,
For my faith, my family,
My caregivers and my friends.

They never told me I would say
"Thank you cancer for all the positives."

They never told me, but I'm telling you now.

IT WAS

It was never "if," it was "when."
BREAST CANCER

It was never "benign," it was always "malignant."
NO SURPRISE

It was a "negative" that through faith
Became a "positive".
OVERCOMING

It was never a "me" battle it was a "shared" fight.
SUPPORT

It was never a "death sentence,"
It is a "learning experience."
ALL IS WELL

HELP

How can you help a person in need?
It can be as simple as a hand held to comfort.
It can be a hug to support.
It can be a smile to lift a spirit.
No words are shared.
There is no visible gift.
There is no reminder to be seen,
Only a shared moment that makes life
Better for the person who receives.

AM I IN THE WRONG OFFICE?

I sit in the waiting room,
Waiting for the multitude of cancer tests prescribed.
I am scheduled for a
PET scan,
BONE scan and
CAT scan.

Wait a minute, am I in the right place?
Is this a veterinarian's office?
I know I would feel so much better,
If my golden retriever were sitting by my side.

ABC's OF CANCER

Attitude helps Beat Cancer.
Deny the disease.
Every day Fight.
God will Help.

Initially Just Keep Level Minded.
Now Operations and Procedures
Quickly Retard cancer's growth
assuring your Survival.

Today Umpteen Valuable Weapons eXist
to fight cancer, adding
Years of Zeal to your life.

C FOR CHRISTMAS, C FOR CANCER, C FOR CELEBRATION

Tis the season of the "C's".
It is Christmas time, a time of celebration,
Yet it is cancer time too, treatments must go on.

Each "C" has its own season.
Christmas is a date on the calendar.
It is a glorious story in the Bible.
It is a season and a reason to live.
Fighting cancer is a season in a life.

Both can be and should be times of celebration,
Because it is during both of these seasons that
The stars are brighter.
The cookies are sweeter.
The cold is crisper.
The smiles are bigger.
The music is more harmonious.
This should be true for one with cancer.

You learn to celebrate every day as if it were
Christmas.
Every day is a gift to be cherished.
Every day is a gift from God.
God, the reason for our celebration,
The reason for each season.

THE CHRISTMAS TREE STORY – THE SYMBOL

The pine, our Christmas tree, the Christian's tree.
It is a symbol of eternal life for it is forever green.
Its very top points and directs us to Heaven.
At Christmas, we decorate this stately symbol.

We place multitudes of lights on its branches.
Just like Christ, the tree becomes
The "Light of the World" in each home.
We place the large bright star on the tree top,
The guiding light to Bethlehem, to Christ and to faith.
We place presents under the tree
Representing the gifts of the Wise men,
And most importantly representing God's greatest gift
To us – his Son, our Christ.

Through him we receive the precious gifts
Of hope, love, peace, and joy.
I smile when I see this most symbolic tree
And think of all it represents.

Isn't it fitting that Christ died on a "wooden" cross?
Maybe, just maybe, it was made from a stately pine.

THE GIFT

A gift is so special.
It starts as a thought, an idea to celebrate,
To raise spirits, to bring a smile, to show you care.
A gift can be purchased or it can be created
By the caring hands of a friend.
It is a gift from the heart, a gift from the soul.
It is something more than special. The idea comes alive.

What starts as a loving thought
Begins with one circle of color,
Wrapped around the needles of the creator.
Does our Creator have a hand in its making?
He helps guide as the needles click together,
And one loop turns into many.

With much time the colors emerge and it grows,
Warming all along the way.
It is held together by love, by hope, by prayer.
When finished, the stitches are cast off,
The fringe is added and knotted,
Holding all that is good together.
The gift is given.

Its purpose unfolds, as it is carefully unwrapped.
It is draped and wrapped around my shoulders,
Soft and warm, comforting the body and the mind.
It is as if God sent his angels and their wings
To confirm his love,
As well as the love of my friend.
The warmth transcends beyond the body into the soul.

What is so beautiful to the eye
Is so much more valuable to the heart.
I am cuddled in blessings.

The gift, the prayer shawl,
Is a constant, comforting hug,
From God, my creator
And from my cherished friend, its creator.
With my love and deepest appreciation: I Thank You.

'TWAS THE DAY OF CHEMOTHERAPY

'Twas the day of chemotherapy.
And all through the house,
Not a creature is stirring,
Not even a mouse.

I get up early,
And jump out of bed,
Fill my bags with food and drinks,
And books to be read.

I eat breakfast of mashed potatoes,
And drink lots of drinks,
They coat and soothe my stomach,
And combat the drugs, I think.

Then it is off to the car,
We go in leaps and bounds,
And we hope the traffic,
Will not slow us I down.

We arrive at the cancer center,
I admit with little glee,
There is a group in the waiting room,
Ready for their chemotherapy.

First it is a blood test,
And then back to the room,
We are greeted by nurses,
It is anything but gloom.

We look around,
And who do we see,
Anita, Lori, Cindy, Nancy,
And our little Suzie.

Nurses Melanie and Brenda,
Are mixing drugs in the back,
We get comfy in our chairs
And we get ready for our snacks.

The bags are hung,
On the poles with care,
In hopes that the cancer cells,
Soon won't be there.

There is Pam in her kerchief,
And I in my wig cap,
And we both settle down,
For our Benadryl nap.

For the next few hours,
We sleep, read and write,
And most importantly,
It is the cancer cells we fight.

We move about very little,
It's not like a home,
It's only to the bathroom,
My pole and I roam.

We see Dr. DeGreen,
A right jolly old elf,
And I laugh when I see him,
In spite of myself.

We spy Dr. Sinor,
And our dear Dr. Kane,
They work hard to make us better,
Making sure we are in no pain.

It takes several hours,
So we make many friends,
We meet once a week,
Six months or so before it ends.

We become family,
The nurses and the people we sit near,
We give support, add advice,
And lend a listening ear.

We'll see you next week,
When we continue the fight,
Then we jump into the car,
And drive out of sight.

I say a prayer for my friends,
As we go down the drive,
My Christmas wish this year,
Is that we all will survive.

So Merry Christmas, best wishes,
And lots of good cheer,
And to my doctors, nurses & friends,
See you next year.

I WILL BE READY

Dear heavenly Father, when You call I will be ready.
I will timidly join You for supper,
For I am ready to drink Your wine and eat Your bread.

I long to sit at Your feet and hear Your words.
I am ready to leave the Christian childhood
And be blessed by maturity.

I will joyfully join Your choir
For I am ready to sing Your praises,
"Hosanna in the Highest" and "Amazing Grace."

I will gladly sprout angelic wings,
I am ready to be a guardian angel
To watch and protect the earthly souls.

Dear heavenly Father, when You are ready,
I will be ready too.

GENERATIONAL DIFFERENCES

I'm not a historical scholar
But I know times have changed.
I grew up in the 50's and 60's.
Life was simpler then. There weren't so many choices.

There was a Buick, a Chevrolet or a Ford.
There were few TVs and even fewer channels.
Life and the shows were all about the family.
There was *Donna Reed, Leave It To Beaver,*
My Three Sons and *Lassie.*

I remember shows about the happy housewife,
The perfect mother,
In her dress and apron baking
Whenever there was a problem.

Oprah and Dr. Phil weren't around
For council and therapy.
I remember one phone
In the central hallway of our house,

But I don't remember it ringing,
Never the endless conversations of today.
It was a time of little communication.
Feelings weren't expressed, just suppressed.

Everything was made to seem perfect.
You didn't know anyone divorced,
Everyone seemed happy.
Psychiatrists were only for the crazies in the world.

Problems were swept under the rug,
Never to be brought up to the surface.
They had to exist, just never talked about.
Life couldn't have, it just couldn't have been that easy.

ME

I talk.
I journal.
I write.
I need to express my feelings.
I need people to know what's inside my heart,

What makes me, me,
What makes me different,
What makes me have a purpose in life,
What makes me important,
What will make me be remembered,
By family I never meet.

CHOCOLATE

It is February.
No better time for a chocolate festival
In the oncology office.

Nothing goes better with a chemo cocktail
Than chocolate.
Chocolate cake, chocolate candy,
Chocolate covered strawberries and pretzels.

It is a sweet and delicious time,
Spent with sweet and caring friends.
Hurray for chocolate! Hurray for life!

THURSDAYS WITH JESSICA

There is a book on the best sellers chart
Entitled "Tuesdays With Morrie."
It is about life lessons shared
Between a former student and a dying professor.

I am blessed to have Thursdays with Jessica.
She is a radiant star, a ray of hope
In life and the chemotherapy room.

We talk. We laugh.
We have blood competition. We share stories.
And yes, we share the battle of breast cancer.

She is a "stay at home mom,"
The almost extinct dinosaur of today.
Three small boys have the privilege of calling her mom.

She is there at the bus stop
To meet and greet and to love,
And she makes a difference in the lives
Of her children and the world around her.
She is a loving, supportive wife, a hunter's widow.
Need I say more?

She is beautiful, not as a super model,
But in the way that counts, both inside and out.
She is always giving, her crafts as gifts,
Her smiles of encouragement,
Her hugs of support.

She is filled with faith and His hope.
I look forward to my Thursdays with Jessica.
She is one of the good things about cancer.
We have learned life lessons together.

Morrie, I know that you are in heaven
And you can save a place for Jessica,
But don't expect her any time soon.
She is needed here on earth.
She is a survivor and
She has too much to live for.

TODAY A SMILE

Today is yesterday's dream of tomorrow.
How many todays do any of us have?
Today, today is a much more vibrant word
Than yesterday or tomorrow.

It is neither the past nor the future, it is the now.
Today is all that is important, all that is promised.
Live today well.
"Assuring a Smile on Your Face."

Yes, even with cancer you can smile
And laugh and have fun.
But, you must allow this to happen.
You must surround yourself
With supportive, loving and laughing people,
Upbeat family and friends –
So wondrous for the curves in your mouth.

Make sure you have a bottle of Windex.
I learned about this from a movie
"My Big Fat Greek Wedding".
You spray it on anything that hurts.
It is just so silly that it works.

Could this be mind over matter?
Fill your senses with fun.
Go to the movies, comedies of course,
And laugh until your stomach hurts.
Take the Windex if needed.

134

Watch funny shows on TV,
Read the comics in the paper.
Your books should be upbeat stories;
Romances and mysteries are acceptable.
Make sure that the Bible is close by.

Try not to worry about the extra pounds
Throughout cancer treatments.
Go out to lunch with skinny friends
Or friends not on diets.
Eat anything that looks good.

Always journal anything funny that happens to you
In bold letters
That are easily found and often read.

Laughter truly is the best medicine.
It will put a smile on your face
And a smile on your heart too.

GRAY

Gray, what a yucky color,
If you can call it a color at all.
It is what you wear when you want to blend in.
It has no pizzazz, no wow power.

Gray days make me cranky,
And when clustered together
Can pull me down into a depression.

There is a reason kids and adults too draw smiley faces,
On the sun in their pictures.
The sun equates to happiness,
Happiness that eludes us on a gray day.

The gray hairs on my head
Never fell out throughout cancer treatments.
They seem to snicker at me in the mirror.
"Just try to make me disappear,
I can beat hair color and drugs."

Sometimes gray is just too powerful to fight.
Gray must be the color of cancer and chemotherapy.

SEXY

When going through cancer treatments
You are not yourself.
You feel bloated.
You feel fat.

Your hair on your head is gone.
Your eyelashes are gone.
Your eyebrows are gone.

You feel anything but beautiful.
You feel anything but sexy.
You feel anything but desirable.

Holding hands becomes intimate.
The physical and emotional scars remain.

THE LORD SPEAKS

"All must come to me as a child.
A child's mind is uncluttered.
They are ready to learn
My faith lessons for spiritual lives.
Their hearts are open to my love.
They are ready to invite me into their daily lives.
Their world is full of fun and games.
I offer the ultimate game to play.
You, my dear children will be the seekers,
And I, your Lord, will be the sought."

LUAU IN PA

We stand at the window.
Outside it is gray and gloomy and cold.
Not to worry, soon we will be at a Luau.

Off we go, clothed in tropical shirts
Only tourists would wear,
And sunglasses in hand.

We arrive. First we see palm trees
And pools of tropical fish.
Then we see the smiling faces.

We are greeted with hugs
And leis are draped over our heads. Aloha!
Everywhere there is color.

Everywhere there is food for the palate,
Fresh pineapples and drinks with paper umbrellas.
What fun!

Who would know we are waiting
For our weekly chemotherapy drugs.
We have been given an escape, a small vacation,
From what could be a day of doom and gloom.

The nurses treat us to a PA Luau
To raise our spirits. And it works!

Thank you our dear caregivers for all you do.
Our hearts and souls are touched.
Smiles are everywhere!

THURSDAY AND THE GANG

We know there are seven days in the week.
We work for the fun and the relaxation
Of the weekend, our special Saturday and Sunday.
Monday is the beginning of the typical work cycle,
Wednesday is the "hump" day
And Friday we start to celebrate.
That leaves Tuesday and Thursday.
For most, they are days with no identity.

But for a gang at the Cancer Center,
Thursdays have become special.
What could be a dreaded day
Has turned into a time of shared stories
And laughter and a raising of spirits.

A group of strangers have bonded together
In friendship, fighting a common enemy.
There are three generations of warriors
That are represented in the circle,
All with different backgrounds
But with one common cause, to beat cancer.

In a short time we have become more than friends,
We have become family.
Together we fight. Together we unite.
Together we have hope. Together we encourage.
Together we make the terrible, tolerable.

We sit in a circle but before long it resembles a circus.
Every circus must have its ringleaders.
We are lucky to have
The most caring nurses who take charge.
Our poles that hold the drugs
Are gaily decorated for each season,

And each season has a reason to celebrate.
There is Halloween with costumes and candy,
Christmas with food and fun,
A Luau to warm and brighten January,
And a chocolate festival for February.

Thank you so very much
For providing us with an atmosphere,
Filled with light and laughter and love and life!
Because of everyone in the room,
The caregivers and friends,
Our fears and anxieties are lessened.
Smiles can only help improve the quality of life.

Over time something has happened to these strangers,
Once quiet victims.
We are warriors. We are heroes. We are survivors.

Hurray for Thursday!
It has become a very special day.
Now we only have to feel sorry for Tuesday.

LAUGHTER

Laughter can be the best medicine.
Laughter can be the best coping mechanism.
Laughter can help heal.
Laughter can be contagious.

If you don't know how to truly laugh,
You don't know what it is like to be truly serious.
They go hand in hand.
So laugh often.

It feels good and it is free.

UNMATCHED PAIR

Bonnie and Clyde.
Ozzie and Harriet.
Romeo and Juliet.
Regis and Kelly.
Grace and Mercy.

What? You've never heard of this famous couple?
They are the names of my breasts.
Now an unmatched pair, as different as day and night.
But close friends nonetheless.

MY 'IST' WORLD

There standing before me, an old friend,
One I haven't seen for years.
She asks what I've been up to?
How do I spend my time?

I ponder a moment.
Recently I've had some basic training
In the medical field.
I go to so many doctors and I go for so many tests.
My days are filled with appointments.

I have an oncologist, a radiologist, a gynecologist,
A pulmonologist, a hemotologist, a dentist,
An ophthamologist, a pharmacist,
A surgeon and a family doctor.

How did they get left out of the IST world?
Wait, they can be called
The specialist and the generalist.
Now the IST list is complete.

Not bad for someone who never had
The measles or chicken pox as a child,
And has been the picture of health,
Barely ever catching a cold as an adult.
Now I spend my time being the patient
In an IST world.

A MOTHERLESS CHILD

Fear of getting sick.
Fear of doctors.
Fear of surgery.
Fear of hospitals.
Fear of needles in veins.
Fear of cancer.
Fear of chemotherapy drugs.
Fear of invisible radiation.
Fear of living.
Fear of dying.

But most of all,
Fear of creating a motherless child.

AGAIN

A bad penny will return.
A boomerang comes back.
A "U" turn takes you to the starting point.
Cancer, not the athlete, makes a comeback.

Cancer strikes again.
We are back at the beginning.
We have to start all over again.
Do I have the energy and strength to fight again?
Again, and again, and again.

MALIGNANT

I hang up the phone.
For a brief moment the laughter is quieted.
The smile fades.
The breathing is shallow.
The eyes cloud.
Malignant.

RE-DIAGNOSED

Cancer is re-diagnosed.
I will not give up for I have a purpose on earth.
I have too much to do, so much to live for.
I have so many reasons to be alive.

I will not give in, give in to a senseless disease.
This disease will not consume my days,
My energy, my thoughts, my being.
Cancer is not who I am.

QUIET

My voice full of laughter is quieted.
My heart full of love and life now quietly beats.
My spirit full of joy lies quietly
Under a blanket of sadness.
Just give me one day in sorrow
And then I will shout again.

A DIFFERENT FOCUS

A decade ago I first faced cancer's woes.
More than the disease, I feared the treatments.
It was as if the IV drugs were the enemy,
Not the over-zealous cells in my body.

I was young and I fought my worst enemy,
The fear of chemo, and I survived.
Treatment complete. I felt stronger.

There was a sense of pride,
As I put that chapter behind me
And I continued on with my life.
Never wanting to think of cancer again.

I wasn't interested in support or help groups.
I had learned my life's lessons.
Or so I thought...
Until I was humbled once again many years later.
Oh how different I am this time around.

God has taken my fears away.
I have a new focus, a new purpose.
It is to help others fight, to raise spirits,
To make people laugh,

To share God's love and to show
The door is open not closed.
All life on earth is a terminal experience,
But there is a promise of eternity.

I'll share my story of hope with anyone who will listen.
Your door can be opened.

I AM FROM

I am from my mother who was little and mighty,
A lover of golf, a maker of chicken divan
And strawberry trifle,
And a breast cancer statistic.

I am from my father who was full of laughter,
Who appeared larger than life,
Was an unbelievable tenor and musician,
A connoisseur of cigars, a buyer at garage sales
And auctions, a purchaser of new cars,
Antique cars and fire trucks,
And a survivor of a broken heart.

I am a part of my sisters' thoughts and feelings.
They were a mystery because of distance
In time and space.

New-found friendships were created
And bonds developed from shared pains and joys.
We have a deep love
For we are all we have from the past.

And they are only a phone call away.
I am who I am because of all of them.

SMILING ANGELS

They used to be the wearers of white,
The angels of hope and healing
For the sick and diseased.
They still wear their wings but
Bright vibrant colors have replaced the white.
Patterned smocks, often seasonal,
Send the message of cheer to all.
The tone in the room is set.

All day long they mix
And administer the chemotherapy drugs.
All day long they stick the veins for the IV's.
Despite everything, they smile.

Bags on poles are changed,
The beeping machines are checked,
All in clockwork fashion.

Something else happens in this room.
Nurses and patients become friends.
It is hard not to get emotionally involved.
Hearts connect.

Time together can be short or it can be long.
But all life is finite.
How difficult it is to accept
When you lose one of yours to cancer.
Yet they still smile.

Pictures of brave, fallen warriors
And victorious gladiators adorn the hallways,
Proof of how special and how fragile life can be.

Beautiful angel statues, thank you gifts,
Sit on the counter,
Tokens of gratitude from loving patients.

Our appreciation for these nurses
Goes beyond gifts and beyond words.
I often wonder why they choose
This profession and this venue,
When other avenues would be so much easier.

Maybe because they are truly
The nurses of hope in this world, chosen angels.
And these angels continue to smile.
And we smile with them.
We smile because of them.

GRADUATION DAY

Today is the day I graduate.
There is no Pomp and Circumstance,
No valedictorian, and no speeches.

It is my final day of cancer treatment.
I am both happy and sad, fearful and joyful,
Anxious and confident.
Believe you me, it is scary to walk away.

Just like graduation day a long time ago,
You are afraid, to walk down the aisle,
Out the door and into an unknown world.

You really don't know what lies ahead.
A part of me does not want to leave,
Not because I always had a good time,
But because I made a good time out of what I had to do.
Believe you me, it is sad to walk away.

I leave behind my team of doctors and nurses
And friends, fellow fighters.
I want to believe that relationships
Will always be the same.
I know that is impossible.

Yet this is supposed to be a time
Of celebration with my friends.
I toss my graduation cap into the air.
I cherish our last party together.

Believe you me, this graduation day, I'll walk away
With joy and gratitude in my heart,
And a tear in my eye.
And I smile when I think of our class reunions.

PATCHWORK QUILT

I look at my body in the mirror.
It reminds me of a patchwork quilt.
Each part is colored fabric
Representing a chapter in my life's battle with cancer.

When I gaze at the reflection,
I see various hues of beige created from radiation,
And patterns emerge from the rounds of surgery.
All the material in the quilt, my body,
Is stitched together with threads of love.

I always marvel when I look at a quilt
And I am, in a way, a medical marvel.
I am a surgeon's work of art
Just like a quilter's masterpiece.
I am my own patchwork quilt.

In time it will wear out and no longer be of service.
But until then it is warm and snuggly and has a purpose.

THE CURE

Will there ever be a cure for cancer?
Is it a promise or a dream?
Is it a scientific fiction novel?

I think about how valuable I am
After six surgeries, expensive treatments,
And countless tests.
The dollar amount must be staggering.

I think about the hundreds of people that are employed,
Because of my battle with cancer.
And I'm only one person in this world.

If a cure for cancer would be found,
The economy of this country,
Would take a massive setback.
It may be even terminal just like cancer can be.

ADJUSTABLE BANGS

I have no eyebrows to pluck.
I have no eyelashes to elongate with mascara.
I always have smooth legs, no stubbles.

The hair on my head never needs cut or restyled.
In fact, when my bangs are in my eyes,
I simply readjust my wig.

There are definite advantages to chemotherapy.
I'll still be glad when it is over
And I make my return to the salon.

ANGER

Anger.
It is not OK.
It will never be OK.
This is senseless.
A door is slammed shut never to open again.
I am angry.

I WILL BE HERE

Someday I will be gone.
When I am gone, I trust I will remain
Alive in your heart.
I want you to believe
That I will be with you always.
I want you to know I will cradle you in arms
You cannot see or feel.

I will always be here.
I want you to know I will surround you
Throughout each and every day.
I will be the morning mist on your face
And the dew on your feet.
I will be the warmth of the afternoon sun
And finally I will be the cool refreshing
Breeze of the evening.

I will always be here.
Please don't make me the tears on your cheek,
But rather the smile on your face.
Smile because I will always be here.
One day we will again be united.
Together we will continue to veil and protect
Those we love and cherish.

We will be unseen yet alive,
Because through death
We are living the promise of believers.
Together we will always be here.
We will all meet again.
Together again!

FLY

We were born to die.
We were designed with wings to fly.
Wings to take us to Heaven
To be united with our Father.
What a glorious journey.
What a joyful flight.

We are now released from the weights of the world.
We are free, flying to our ultimate destination,
Our predestined home.
It is time to rejoice and fly.

ANOTHER CHAPTER ENDED

Another chapter in our battle
Against cancer has concluded.

I say "our" because it is not "my" battle.
My husband and my family
Have felt every bit of the pain I have endured.
My friends have been a source of encouragement
Each and every day.
Our Father God has been
A guiding light in so many ways.

Good does come from bad.
You just have to be patient,
To see which doors are closed
And which doors are opened.

If you added all the negatives from cancer,
They would fill a teaspoon.
Cancer's positives I've experienced,
What I have learned about myself,
About my faith and about life, would fill a cup.
Right now, my cup runneth over.